MILK & DAIRY PRODUCTS

HEALTHY EATING

BY GEMMA M^cMULLEN

CONTENTS

©2016
Book Life
King's Lynn
Norfolk PE30 4LS

ISBN: 978-1-910512-44-9

Written by:
Gemma McMullen
Edited by:
Harriet Brundle
Designed by:
Drue Rintoul & Ian McMullen

A catalogue record for this book is available from the British Library.

Look out for the underlined words in this book, they are explained in the glossary on page 24.

WHAT ARE MILK AND DAIRY PRODUCTS?

Milk is a white liquid made by the bodies of some animals. Milk can be drunk or used to make food for humans. Most of the milk that we use comes from cows.

Dairy products are made from milk. They include cheese and yoghurt.

MILK

Having milk in your diet is important because it helps the body to grow healthy bones and teeth.

Milk can be used as a drink. It is often put with cereal.

Adults put milk in hot drinks such as tea.

WHERE DOES MILK COME FROM?

Milk is made by cows. Farmers keep dairy cows especially for their milk. On large farms, special machines take the milk from the cows.

The milk is prepared by special machines before it is bottled for use.

Milk needs to be kept cold in the fridge.

CHEESE

Cheese is a product made using milk. It is made in special <u>factories</u> and takes quite a long time to produce.

There are lots of different types of cheese, each with different flavours.

Cheese has a longer shelf-life than milk.

YOGHURT

Yoghurt is a product made using milk. Natural yoghurt is sour in taste, so yoghurt is often sweetened before it is sold.

Yoghurt can be sweetened with fruit or honey but sweetened yoghurt often contains a lot of sugar.

BUTTER

Butter is a dairy product. Milk is <u>churned</u> to separate the fat from the milk. Butter is made using the fat.

Butter is often used as a spread or as a baking ingredient.

HEALTHY DAIRY PRODUCTS

Milk and dairy products are good for our bodies because they contain important proteins and minerals such as calcium.

Some dairy products contain lots of fats or sugars. These products are best eaten as treats.

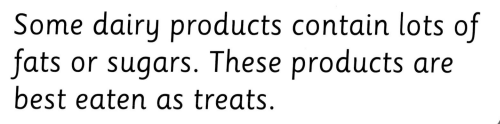

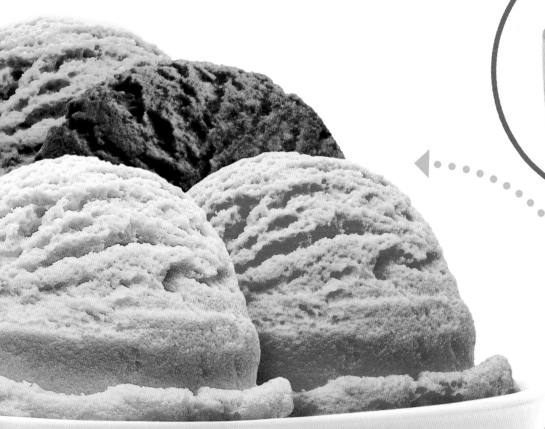

Ice-cream has a lot of fat in it.

OTHER MILK SOURCES

Lots of animals make milk to feed their babies. Cows' milk is mostly used for food and drinks but some other animals' milk can also be used.

Goats' milk and sheep's milk are both safe to drink.

MILK FROM OTHER ANIMALS

Water Buffaloes are the main source of milk in South Asia.

Camels' milk is said to have up to ten times the iron found in cows' milk.

Yaks' milk is high in fat making it good for yoghurt, butter and cheese.

Reindeer milk is popular in northern regions.

21

CHEESE FROM AROUND THE WORLD

Mozarella is a cheese from Italy. It is quite springy to touch.

Marscapone also comes from Italy. It is used in sweet dishes such as cheesecake. It is also used in savoury dishes.

Cheddar cheese is an English cheese. It is pale yellow and feels hard.

Roquefort is a French cheese. In France it is called 'the cheese of kings'.

23

GLOSSARY

churned
spun until products separate

factories
buildings where things are made

minerals
substances in our bodies which keep us healthy

proteins
substances in our bodies which help us to grow

shelf-life
how long a food item stays fresh

INDEX